CREEPY CREATURES
MUMMIES

Big Buddy Books
An Imprint of Abdo Publishing
abdopublishing.com

Sarah Tieck

abdopublishing.com

Published by Abdo Publishing, a division of ABDO, PO Box 398166, Minneapolis, Minnesota 55439.
Copyright © 2016 by Abdo Consulting Group, Inc. International copyrights reserved in all countries. No part
of this book may be reproduced in any form without written permission from the publisher. Big Buddy Books™
is a trademark and logo of Abdo Publishing.

Printed in the United States of America, North Mankato, Minnesota.
042015
092015

THIS BOOK CONTAINS
RECYCLED MATERIALS

Cover Photo: Zens photo/Getty Images.
Interior Photos: ASSOCIATED PRESS (pp. 9, 11, 13, 17, 22); Deposit Photos (p. 29); Glow Images (pp. 15, 23);
     ©iStockphoto.com (pp. 7, 9, 19, 25, 30); Shutterstock.com (pp. 5, 11, 27); Time Life Pictures/Getty Images
     (p. 20); Universal Pictures/Getty Images (p. 21); © ZUMA Press, Inc/Alamy (p. 20).

Coordinating Series Editor: Rochelle Baltzer
Contributing Editors: Megan M. Gunderson, Bridget O'Brien, Marcia Zappa
Graphic Design: Jenny Christensen

Library of Congress Cataloging-in-Publication Data

Tieck, Sarah, 1976-
  Mummies / Sarah Tieck.
     pages cm. -- (Creepy creatures)
  ISBN 978-1-62403-766-5
1. Mummies--Juvenile literature. I. Title.
  GN293.T54 2016
  393'.3--dc23
                         2015002208

Contents

Creepy Mummies

People love to tell spooky stories, especially about creepy creatures such as mummies. They describe mummies as coming back to life. And, they report unusual events happening. Could it be a mummy's curse?

Mummies have appeared in books, stories, plays, television shows, and movies. But are they real, or the stuff of **legend**? Let's find out more about mummies, and you can decide for yourself!

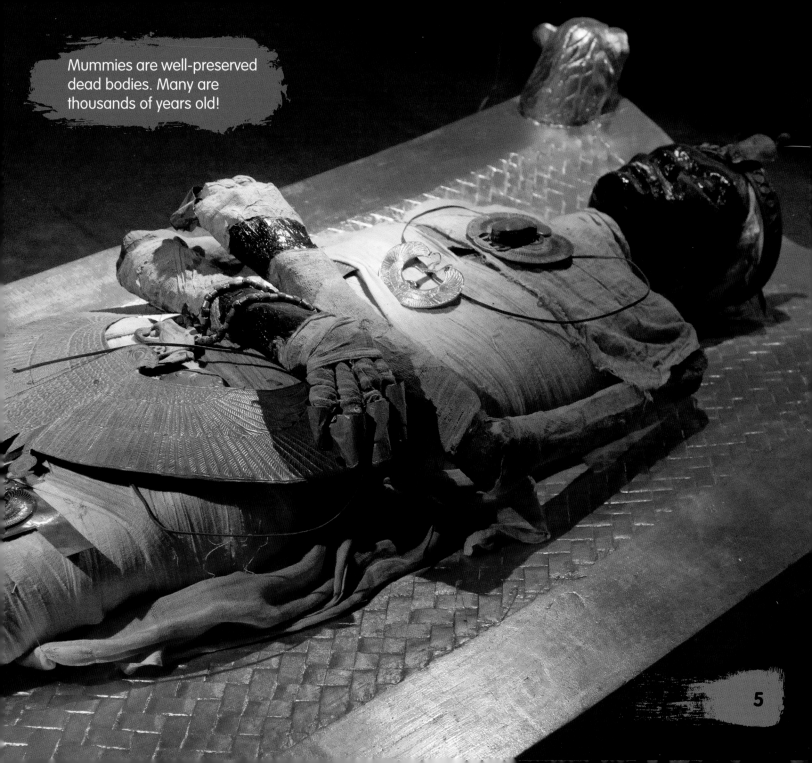

Mummies are well-preserved dead bodies. Many are thousands of years old!

Scary Stories

Mummies are found around the world. They are discovered in deserts, mountains, and caves. Sometimes, they are wrapped in layers of cloth.

Stories describe mummies as coming back to life. Some mummies are brought to life using a **spell**. Others come to life accidentally when their resting place is bothered.

Did you know?

After coming back to life, some mummies change to look more like they did when they were alive.

Mummies may be upset and want to harm people when they are awakened.

In many stories, people who find mummies become sick or even die. This can happen when a mummy is angry that its body was moved or that its **tomb** was opened. Sometimes this is caused by a curse on the mummy or its tomb.

Mummies may move slowly because their bodies are very old. But, these monsters are nearly impossible to stop. In stories, people use fire or magic to kill them.

Sometimes, a curse is written in stone outside a mummy's tomb. Ancient Egyptians did this using their picture language, called hieroglyphics (heye-ruh-GLIH-fihks).

In 1892, Sir Arthur Conan Doyle printed a short story called "Lot No. 249." It is about an evil mummy that comes to life.

Around the World

Mummies have been found around the world. Thousands of mummies have been found in **peat bogs** in northern Europe. Some are more than 2,500 years old.

The most famous mummies have come from Egypt. In 1922, **archaeologist** Howard Carter found the **tomb** of King Tut in Egypt. King Tut's mummified body had been in the tomb for more than 3,000 years.

People were very interested in Egypt after King Tut's tomb was found!

King Tut's real name was Tutankhamen. He was buried in a gold mask.

11

In the 1400s, the Spanish found thousands of mummies in the Canary Islands. Many were found in caves.

Mummified **Inca** bodies were found in the Andes Mountains in 1999. Their lives ended as part of a special **ritual**. Ice and cold helped turn them into mummies after death. So, they look much like they did when they died.

Inca mummies died high in the mountains. "The Maiden" was around 15 when she died more than 500 years ago.

13

Living History

Bodies can become mummified by **peat bogs**, ice, and cold. But, ancient Egyptians followed specific steps to make mummies. First, they removed the body's blood and many of its **organs**. Then, they preserved the body using dried plants. Finally, they wrapped the body in cloth and placed it in a **coffin**.

Did you know?

Often, ancient Egyptians buried treasures with mummies. They believed this would help the dead in the afterlife.

Sometimes, an ancient Egyptian mummy was placed in a special coffin called a sarcophagus.

15

There are few mummies left today. Grave robbers often stole mummies and the treasures they were buried with. Sometimes, the mummies were ground up for use as medicine. Over time, people began to gather mummies in museums and care for them.

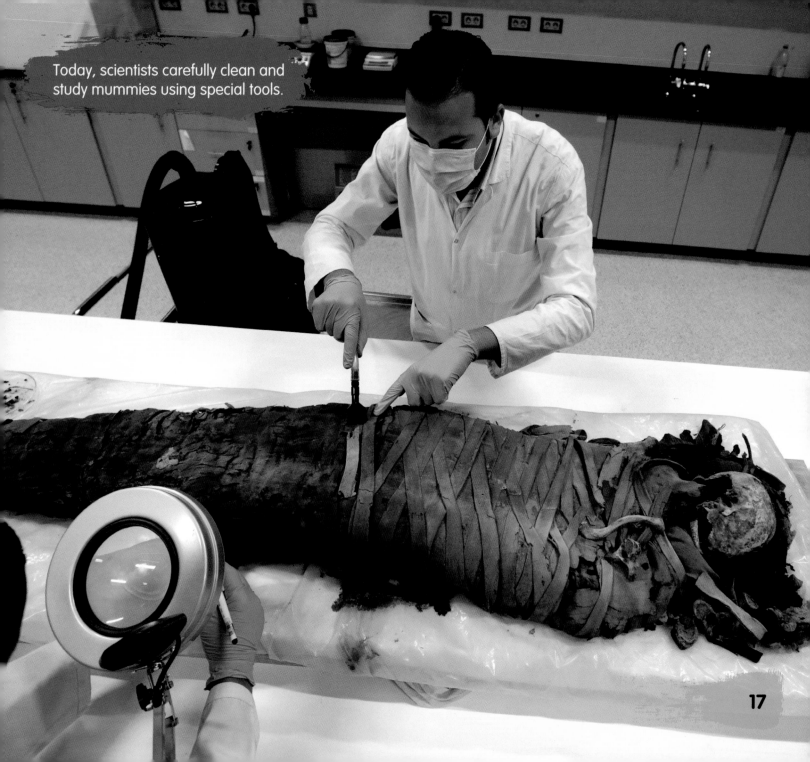

Today, scientists carefully clean and study mummies using special tools.

Good or Evil?

In stories, some mummies are feared monsters. They may have **supernatural** strength or magic powers. People who find a mummy's treasure may get hurt or even die!

In other stories, these monsters are lonely. They may be trying to find someone they have lost. But, people have to find a way to put the mummy to rest again. Sometimes, they must call on ancient gods for help!

Many mummy stories are set in deserts such as the Sahara in Africa.

Queen Tera

In 1903, Bram Stoker's horror book *The Jewel of Seven Stars* was printed. In it, an **archaeologist** and others try to bring the mummy Queen Tera back to life.

Where's My Mummy?

Scooby-Doo and friends solve a mystery in Egypt in this 2005 movie. Velma is helping to fix a famous statue called the Sphinx. While there, they find mummies and Egyptian queen Cleopatra's **tomb**.

Mummies in Pop Culture

Kharis

This living mummy appeared in the movie *The Mummy's Hand* in 1940. He guarded the **tomb** of Egyptian princess Ananka for 3,000 years. His story continued in three more movies.

Im-Ho-Tep

Actor Boris Karloff played an Egyptian mummy in the 1932 movie *The Mummy*. Im-Ho-Tep is brought to life after more than 3,500 years. He searches for his lost love.

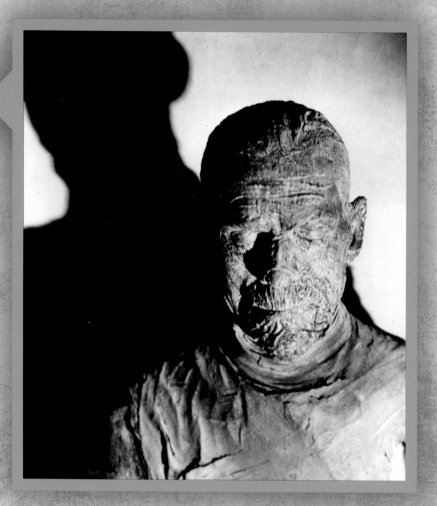

Imhotep

The exciting 1999 movie *The Mummy* is a remake of the 1932 film. In it, **archaeologists** fight living mummy Imhotep. Several related movies and television shows followed.

Did you know?

The Mummy Chronicles series by Dave Wolverton is set in 1937. In these books, 12-year-old Alex O'Connell fights mummies and curses in Egypt. Alex is a character in 1999's *The Mummy*.

Fact or Fiction?

Mummy curses are common in stories, but most people today don't believe in them. Scientists have studied ancient **tombs**. In some, they have found dangerous matter that could make people sick. But, there is no proof that this caused people to become sick and die.

Still, scientists say that mummy curses are not real. They say the stories of deaths caused by curses were probably started by **rumors**. People became afraid and news reports made their fear worse.

When discovered, some tombs have been sealed for hundreds of years. There may be lots of dust. Scientists protect themselves with gloves and masks.

Many mummified bodies have been destroyed or lost. But, some remain in museums or in science labs. Some mummies have hair on their heads. Others still have food in their stomachs! Scientists study mummies to learn about life in the past.

Did you know?

The Field Museum in Chicago, Illinois, has one of the largest collections of mummies in the United States. There is even a three-story model of a tomb.

Mummies make popular museum displays.

What Do You Think?

So, what do you think about mummies? Do they still send a chill up your spine? It can be fun to watch spooky mummy movies or to dress as a mummy on Halloween.

It is also interesting to learn about real mummies. Knowing what is true and what is made up is powerful. Whether you read **fiction** about mummies or discover their real-life history, you are in for an interesting journey.

A mummy Halloween costume can be made using bandages, cloth strips, or even toilet paper!

Let's Talk

What examples of mummy stories can you think of?

What would you do if you had to fight a mummy's curse?

How do you think it would feel to be an explorer and find a mummy?

If you were to write a story about a mummy, what special powers would your mummy have?

Imagine you are a king or queen of ancient Egypt. What do you think it would be like to come to life as a mummy thousands of years later?

Glossary

archaeologist (ahr-kee-AH-luh-jihst) a person who studies human activities of the past.

coffin a box in which a dead person is buried.

fiction stories that are not real.

Inca South American Indians who ruled a large empire until 1535.

legend an old story that many believe, but cannot be proven true.

organ a body part that does a special job. The heart and the lungs are organs.

peat bog soft, wet land filled with material formed by the remains of decaying plants.

ritual (RIH-chuh-wuhl) a formal act or set of acts that is repeated.

rumor a story that is passed from person to person but has not been proven to be true.

spell words with magic powers.

supernatural unable to be explained by science or nature.

tomb (TOOM) a special building or structure that houses the dead.

Websites

To learn more about Creepy Creatures, visit **booklinks.abdopublishing.com**. These links are routinely monitored and updated to provide the most current information available.

Index